PUCCINI
Two Arias from La Rondine
FOR SOPRANO

Translations and Plot Synopses
by Martha Gerhart

COVER ILLUSTRATION: ROBERT NELSON

ISBN 978-0-7935-1571-4

HAL•LEONARD®
CORPORATION
7777 W. BLUEMOUND RD. P.O. BOX 13819 MILWAUKEE, WI 53213

LA RONDINE (The Swallow) was first performed on March 27, 1917 in Monte Carlo. The Italian verse of the libretto is by Giuseppe Adami, from an original libretto in German by Alfred Willner and Heinz Reichert. The opera (or operetta) takes place in the 1850s, or sometime during the Second Empire of Napoleon III (1851-1870).

La Canzone di Doretta
(Chi il bel sogno)

from Act I
setting: an elegantly furnished salon in Magda's Paris home

Act I opens directly on a spirited party hosted by Magda de Civry, mistress of the wealthy banker Rambaldo Fernandez. Magda is pouring after-dinner coffee. Her girlfriends enjoy mocking Prunier, a poet, for his view that romantic love has become fashionable in Paris. At Magda's bidding, Prunier sits at the piano and begins ("Chi il bel sogno di Doretta potè indovinar?") the story of his latest creation, a heroine he named Doretta, for whom a king's gold could not bring happiness; but Prunier doesn't know how to finish the story. Magda, attracted to the tale because of her dream of true love, takes Prunier's place at the piano and rapturously completes it with her own verse.

Although the solo piano introduction is actually played by Prunier in the scene as the introduction to his story, it sets the appropriate mood for Magda's verse as traditionally excerpted for concert or audition, and is included in this edition. In performance of the complete opera, the party guests add rhythmically spoken comment as Magda sings.

Chi il bel sogno di Doretta potè indovinar?	*Who could guess Doretta's beautiful dream?*
Il suo mister come mai finì?	*How did its mystery end?*
Ahimè! un giorno uno studente	*Alas, one day a student*
in bocca la baciò,	*kissed her lips,*
e fu quel bacio rivelazione:	*and that kiss was revelation:*
Fu la passione!	*It was passion!*
Folle amore! Folle ebbrezza!	*Frenzied love! Frenzied rapture!*
Chi la sottil carezza	*Who could ever describe*
d'un bacio così ardente	*the subtle caress of a*
mai ridir potrà?	*kiss so ardent?*
Ah! mio sogno! Ah! mia vita!	*Ah, my dream! Ah, my life!*
Che importa la ricchezza	*Of what importance is wealth*
se alfin è rifiorita la felicità!	*if, at last, happiness has blossomed again!*
O sogno d'or poter amar così!	*Oh golden dream, to be able to love like that!*

Ore dolci e divine

from Act I
setting: the same, moments later

As Rambaldo joins his men friends in the winter garden for a smoke, Magda's girlfriends (Bianca, Suzy and Yvette) join her to express their envy of her comfortable life with Rambaldo. Magda protests that money is not all-important; she begins a reminiscence ("Ore dolci e divine") of what happened on the first evening she left her aunt's home as an innocent young woman. On that evening, at Bullier's, she was infatuated with a man she never saw again. In the score, Magda's girlfriends interpolate some enthusiastic comments not included in this solo presentation of the aria.

The Bal Bullier (Bullier's dance hall) was situated until 1957 on the Avenue de l'Observatoire in Paris. One of the most popular places for Bohemian socializing during the Second Empire, it was frequented by the famous courtesans and coquettes as well as by literary figures such as Henri Mürger and Théodore de Banville.

"Bocks" are very strong beers, in mugs or glasses, popular in French cafés. A "bock beer" derives its name from *Ambockbier,* in the French pronunciation of the German *Einbeckbier,* i.e., beer from Einbeck.

Ore dolci e divine	Sweet and divine hours
di lieta baraonda	of gay commotion
fra studenti e sartine	among students and seamstresses
d'una notte a Bullier!	of a night at Bullier's!
Come andai? Non lo so!	How did I go there? I don't know!
Come uscii? Non lo so!	How did I leave? I don't know!
Cantava una lenta canzone la musica strana,	The strange music sang a slow song,
e una voce lontana diceva così:	and a distant voice spoke like this:
«Fanciulla, è sbocciato l'amore!	"Maiden, love has been born!
Difendi il tuo cuore!	Defend your heart!
Dei baci e sorrisi l'incanto	The enchantment of kisses and smiles
si paga con stille di pianto!»	is paid for with teardrops!"
Quando ci sedemmo, stanchi,	When we sat down, tired,
estenuati dalla danza,	exhausted from the dancing,
la gola arsa,	throats parched,
ma l'anima piena d'allegrezza,	but souls full of cheer,
mi parve che si schiudesse tutta una nuova esistenza!	it seemed to me that a whole new existence was unfolding!
«Due bocks, » egli disse al garzone!	"Two bocks," he said to the waiter!
Stupita fissavo	Astonished, I stared at
quel grande scialone!	that big spendthrift!
Gettò venti soldi.	He threw down twenty sous.
Aggiunse: «Tenete!»	He added: "Keep it!"
«Piccola adorata mia,	"My little adored one,
il tuo nome vuoi dir?»	do you wish to tell your name?"
Io sul marmo scrissi;	I wrote on the marble;
egli accanto il nome suo tracciò…	he, close-by, traced his name…
E là, fra la mattana	And there, amid the rowdiness
di tutta quella gente,	of all those people,
ci siamo guardati	we gazed at each other,
ma senza dir niente…	but without saying anything…
M'impaurii? Non lo so!	Did I become frightened? I don't know!
Poi fugii! Più non so!	Then I fled! I know no more!
Cantava una triste canzone la musica strana,	The strange music sang a sad song,
e una voce lontana diceva così:	and a distant voice spoke like this:
«Fanciulla, è sbocciato l'amore!	"Maiden, love has been born!
Difendi il tuo cuore!	Defend your heart!
Dei baci e sorrisi l'incanto	The enchantment of kisses and smiles
si paga con stille di pianto!»	is paid for with teardrops!"
Potessi rivivere ancora	Could I but relive again
la gioia d'un'ora!	the joy of one hour!

As the plot continues…

At the end of Act I, Magda decides to go to Bullier's again, dressed as a grisette and calling herself "Paulette." In Act II, the scenario of "Ore dolce e divine" is repeated when, at Bullier's, she falls in love with Ruggero Lastouc, a young man from the country. Son of a friend of Rambaldo, Ruggero had made a brief appearance at the Act I party, receiving advice as to where to best spend his first night in Paris. The recommendation of choice was Buillier's!

The love Magda finds with Ruggero ultimately leads to the denouement of her story. In Act III, having rejected Rambaldo for a life with Ruggero on the Riviera, Magda leaves Ruggero, accepting the fact that her past does not permit her, socially, to become a respected wife in his repected family. Migrating toward "a land of sun and dreams," she is like a swallow who migrates toward the sea. As Prunier predicted in Act I, Magda returns, we assume, to the feathered nest of Rambaldo.

La Canzone di Doretta

from
LA RONDINE

GIACOMO PUCCINI

gior - no u - no stu - den-te in boc - ca la ba - cio e fu quel ba - cio ri - ve-la-zio - ne:

Sostenendo
dolcissimo

Fu la pas - sio - ne! Fol - le a - mo - re!

Fol - le eb - brez - za! Chi la sot - til ca -
cantando

rez - za d'un ba-cio co-sì ar-den - te mai ri - dir po - trà?

Ore dolci e divine
from
LA RONDINE

GIACOMO PUCCINI

Due bocks e - gli dis - se al gar - zo - ne! Stu -

pi - ta fis - sa - vo quel gran - de scia - lo - ne! Get -

tò __ ven - ti sol dì. Ag - giun - se: Te -

ne - te!

molto stacc. e. cresc.

«Pic-co-la a-do-ra - ta mi - a,

rit. *tornando* *a tempo*

Il tuo no - me vuoi dir?»_____ Io sul

rit. *tornando* *a tempo*

mar - mo scris - si: egli ac - can - to il

no - me suo trac - cio...

E là, fra la mat - ta - na di tut - ta quel - la

rall.

Tempo I *(Larghetto)*

gen - te, ci sia - mo guar - da - ti ma sen - za dir

poco rit.

fen - di, di - fen - di, di - fen di il tuo cuo - re! _____ Dei

a tempo

ba - ci e sor - ri - si l'in - can - to _____ si

pa - ga con stil - le, con stil - le di pian - to!» Po -

tes - si ri - vi - ve - re an - co - ra _____

la gio - ia, la gio-ia du-no -

ra! ____ Po - tes - si ____ ri - vi -

ver ____ la gio - ia, la gio-ia du-no -ra!